Faithful Whispers

Becoming Whole Through Faith and Healing

By Tyeisha Kones

© **Copyright 2025 - All rights reserved.**

This content contained within this book may not be reproduced, distributed, or transmitted in any form or by any means, including photocopying, recording, or other electronic or mechanical methods, without the prior written permission of the author, except in the case of brief quotations used in book reviews.

Under no circumstances will any blame or legal responsibility be held against the publisher, or author, for any damage, reparation, or monetary loss due to the information contained within this book, either directly or indirectly.

Disclaimer:

This workbook is for informational and educational purposes only. The author and publisher are not responsible for any results from following the exercises or recommendations within. The content should not be considered professional, legal, or medical advice.

TABLE OF CONTENTS

Introduction
Pages 4–5

Chapter 1: Divine Awakening
Pages 6–10

Chapter 2: The Roots We Didn't Plan –
Pages 11–15

Chapter 3: The Battle Within the Mind
Pages 16–20

Chapter 4: Healing the Inner Child
Pages 21–26

Chapter 5: Making Peace with the Past
Pages 27–30

Chapter 6: Overcoming Negative Thoughts Through God's Truth
Pages 31–35

Chapter 7: Redefining the Soft Girl Era Through Faith
Pages 36–39

Chapter 8: Love, Partnership, & Faith
Pages 40-44

Chapter 9: Parenting from a Healed Place
Pages 45-50

Chapter 10: When God Holds Up the Mirror
Pages 51-54

Chapter 11: Life After Christ
Pages 55-59

Chapter 12: Speak Life – The Power of Our Words
Pages 60-63

Chapter 13: When Their Words Don't Define You
Pages 64-70

Chapter 14: Ask, Don't Assume –
Pages 71-74

Chapter 15: Doing Your Best with What You Have
Pages 75-77

Final Thoughts – A Sacred Surrender
Pages 78-80

Helpful Resources
Pages 81-82

About the Author
Page 83

Acknowledgments
Pages 84-85

Introduction

There was a time in my life when I felt completely broken—mentally, emotionally, and spiritually. I had lost my sense of direction, doubted my worth, and questioned whether healing was even possible for someone like me. But in that silence—between the tears, the setbacks, and the long prayers—I began to hear what I now call faithful whispers. Quiet reminders from God that I was still loved, still chosen, and still capable of becoming whole.

This book was born from those whispers. It is the result of a deeply personal journey— one filled with growth, reflection, and surrender. It wasn't an easy road. There were moments I wanted to give up, times I questioned everything, and seasons where I had to rebuild from the ground up. But with every step, God met me with grace.

"Faithful Whispers" is not just a book— it's an invitation. An invitation to slow down, tune in, and allow God to meet you in your most vulnerable spaces. It's a space where faith meets healing and where you begin to reclaim your peace.

Introduction

Each chapter will walk you through a different stage of the healing journey—from nurturing your inner child to managing anxiety, from building confidence to embracing self-love. You'll read pieces of my story, reflect on your own, and be guided by scriptures.

You don't have to be perfect to begin. You just have to be willing. This book is for anyone who feels tired of carrying pain alone, anyone searching for clarity, and anyone ready to live a softer, more faith-filled life.

Let this be your sacred space. A place to heal, to reflect, and to become who God created you to be.

CHAPTER 1

A DIVINE AWAKENING

> *"This is all the more urgent, for you know how late it is; time is running out. Wake up, for our salvation is nearer now than when we first believed."*— Romans 13:11

As I was taking a shower during my daily prayer, God spoke to me—and His words were loud and clear. I've never been great at speaking my thoughts aloud. For as long as I can remember, I've always had to write to process what I'm feeling. A while ago, I prayed and asked God to help me step into my purpose. I had no idea how or when He would answer, but I kept praying. I knew I was created for something greater—I just didn't know how to access it.

A DIVINE AWAKENING

I remember a few years ago, I was finally starting to feel aligned. I was on the right track. And then, somehow, life happened—and I got thrown off course. But before all of that, I remember vividly telling my best friend, Jalisa, that I wanted to write a book. I had no idea what the book would be about, but I knew I had a story. I felt it deep in my spirit that God needed me to get something out to His people. I just didn't know what to say or how to say it, and over time, the dream got buried.

But recently, God brought it back to the surface.

I published my first self-healing journal, *Faith Journaling: A Reflective Journal for Healing, Growth, and Spiritual Renewal.* And as I began drafting the workbook—writing affirmations, scriptures, and reflective prompts—my mind and spirit began to expand. I started reflecting deeper, listening closer. And now, here I am…writing the very book I once gave up on. This book is no longer about my healing—it's a message. A divine revelation. While in prayer, God spoke again. He revealed to me that the way we are living… is not right.
The way we are parenting… is not right.
This world—this violence, this suicide, this bullying, these mental health crises—this is not normal. He said, "This was never how I intended it to be."

A DIVINE AWAKENING

God made it clear that so much of what we're seeing today can be traced back to one painful root: childhood trauma. That is the thread connecting so many of the struggles we carry silently. This book exists for one reason—to help you unpack that pain. To help you reflect. To guide you to healing. To break the cycles.

Let's take a moment to think about the generations before us.

I'm 27.
My parents are in their late 40s to mid-50s.
My grandparents are in their late 60s to early 70s.
My great-grandparents would've been in their 90s or 100s.

That means my great-grandparents were the beginning of the most recent generational cycle.
What did they experience?

Slavery.
Discrimination.
Extreme poverty.
Rape.
Hard labor.
Physical beatings.
Shame and silence.

A DIVINE AWAKENING

Back then, survival came through silence and suffering. Beatings, yelling, fear-based discipline—that was the norm. And because my grandmother grew up under those conditions and "turned out okay," she believed it was right. But just because something is normalized doesn't mean it's healthy. Those same patterns passed on to her children. Then to theirs. And now…here we are. We've made the brokenness look normal. We've made trauma look like tradition.
And now we have a world of adults, teens, and children acting out unhealed pain—through violence, dysfunction, and emotional disconnection. People are hurting each other because they're carrying pain they were never allowed to process.

But have you noticed something lately?
More people are opting into gentle parenting.
More are choosing therapy.
More are choosing peace over performance.

Something is shifting.

God is calling us to break free.
We must change.
We must heal.
We must pray.
We must let go of the mindset that says, "This was done to me, and I turned out fine."

A DIVINE AWAKENING

Because truthfully… did you really turn out fine? Or are your financial stability, career success, and material possessions just covering wounds that haven't healed?

This is the moment to reflect. To see the bigger picture. To be honest.

Something has to give. God says so.

CHAPTER 2:

**THE ROOTS WE DIDN'T PLANT —
UNDERSTANDING CHILDHOOD TRAUMA**

> *"He heals the brokenhearted and binds up their wounds." — Psalm 147:3*

Let's talk about something that most of us are silently battling yet rarely given the tools or space to name—childhood trauma.

Childhood trauma isn't just about major, obvious events like abuse or neglect. It's also about the subtle, repeated emotional injuries—like feeling unseen, constantly criticized, emotionally abandoned, shamed for your feelings, or being forced to grow up too soon. It's the heartbreak of a child never receiving the love, protection, or nurturing they deserved.

**THE ROOTS WE DIDN'T PLANT —
UNDERSTANDING CHILDHOOD TRAUMA**

For many of us, trauma became the air we breathed. It became our "normal," not because it was right, but because it was familiar. And as children, we adapt. We learn to survive—even when it means silencing ourselves, people-pleasing, or disconnecting from our emotions.

But here's the thing: what we never heal from will find a way to speak in our adult life.

What Is Childhood Trauma?

Childhood trauma is any experience in early life that overwhelms a child's ability to cope with or feel safe. It disrupts the sense of trust, safety, and belonging that all children need to thrive.

It can come in many forms:
• Emotional neglect or inconsistency

• Physical, emotional, or sexual abuse

•Growing up in a home with addiction, violence, or mental illness

• Being bullied, shamed, or constantly criticized
• Experiencing grief, poverty, or homelessness

Sound familiar? That's trauma showing up in disguise.

THE ROOTS WE DIDN'T PLANT — UNDERSTANDING CHILDHOOD TRAUMA

I remember talking to my brother one day about his problems, and I asked him jokingly, "Dang, we must've had different parents." His morals, values, and mindset were so different from mine. Although he's older than me, I found myself doing all the coaching. That conversation taught me something: childhood trauma affects us all differently. It shows up in different ways, even among siblings. It wasn't that we had different parents—we had different perceptions of the same past, and that shaped how we carry it.

I remember him saying, "I've been having a lot of anxiety, like I'm having a panic attack." At that time, he was under a lot of stress. And stress has a way of unleashing those inner child wounds without us even realizing it. Old fears. Old insecurities. Unmet needs. They come to the surface and demand to be felt.

Anxiety isn't weakness—it's often your body asking you to pay attention to what was once ignored.

Why This Chapter Matters

I wrote this chapter not just to inform—but to free you.

THE ROOTS WE DIDN'T PLANT — UNDERSTANDING CHILDHOOD TRAUMA

Because like many of you, I didn't realize I was carrying trauma. I thought being "strong" meant pushing through it. I didn't understand why I felt overwhelmed in relationships or why I couldn't trust love or rest.

But God has been walking me through it.

He's shown me that the dysfunction, violence, and broken parenting cycles we see in the world today often come from generations of trauma that were never healed—only passed down. This is why I created my journal. This is why I'm writing this book. Not just to speak life—but to help you understand why healing is holy.

We Break the Cycle By Naming the Root

You're not "too emotional."
You're not "too broken."
You're not "crazy."
You're responding to wounds you were never allowed to grieve. But here's the truth: you can heal.

"Therefore if anyone is in Christ, the new creation has come: The old has gone, the new is here!" — 2 Corinthians 5:17 (NIV)

THE ROOTS WE DIDN'T PLANT — UNDERSTANDING CHILDHOOD TRAUMA

When we allow God to go to the root, He begins to pull out the lies we were raised on. He replaces them with truth. With grace. With wholeness. And as we heal, we don't just change our lives—we change generations.

CHAPTER 3

THE BATTLE WITHIN THE MIND

> *"Do not conform to the pattern of this world but be transformed by the renewing of your mind." — Romans 12:2*

The mind is a powerful tool. It can be your greatest strength or your biggest weakness—depending on how you use it. It's easy to get trapped in your own thoughts. You've heard the phrase, "My mind is playing tricks on me." That phrase holds so much truth. You are what you believe and what you think. The key to winning in life is learning how to control your mind, not let it control you.

THE BATTLE WITHIN THE MIND

Over the years, I've allowed my mind to convince me that the people I loved were my enemies. My trauma, insecurities, and unresolved pain clouded my perception and caused me to project those emotions onto others. As the saying goes, "hurt people hurt people." And the cycle continues—until we choose to feed our minds with truth, positivity, and God's word.

Once I truly sought God and allowed Him to take the lead in my life, it felt like a switch went off in my mind—like that lightbulb moment you see in cartoons. That was me. When God stepped in, the fog started to lift. Even when negative thoughts crept back in, I began to pray, asking God to wrap His arms around me and bring comfort to my chaos. I would pray for clarity and wisdom, asking Him to show me what He needed me to see, and guide me toward His purpose.

"Trust in the Lord with all your heart and lean not on your own understanding." —Proverbs 3:5

I began to understand that sometimes the intrusive thoughts we have are just unhealed wounds that need our attention. God, in His

THE BATTLE WITHIN THE MIND

divine wisdom will often mirror those wounds in the people around us—not to punish us, but to bring us into realization and transformation. Healing isn't just for us—it's also for our relationship with God.

You ever find yourself asking: "Why is this happening to me?" "What am I doing wrong?" "Why do people always treat me this way?" But God is not a God of confusion—He is direct, intentional, and deeply loving. When we allow Him into our hearts, those questions begin to shift. Instead of asking "Why me?," we begin to ask: "What is God trying to show me?" "What lesson is He teaching me?" "What wounds am I avoiding?"

We often blame others, but the truth is, God doesn't point out our flaws to shame us—He does it to restore us. When we live disconnected from God, we live in a mind full of noise. A life without God isn't just harder—it's empty. And it becomes harder to hear His voice when our heads are full of other voices and distractions. But with God, those voices get quieter.

"My sheep listen to my voice; I know them, and they follow me." — John 10:27

THE BATTLE WITHIN THE MIND

One of the most powerful lines I pray is: *"God, without You, I am nothing. A life without You is not worth living."* That prayer changed my life. When I accepted that truth, life became more joyful. My focus shifted from *"What can this world do for me?"* to *"What can I do for this world?"* I began to live with purpose instead of pain.

We are what makes this world go around. And when we choose healing, when we choose God, we help heal the world. Our light inspires others to shine. This journey is not about comparison. It's not about outshining others. It's about sharing light, spreading love, and walking with purpose.

"Let your light shine before others, that they may see your good deeds and glorify your Father in heaven." — Matthew 5:16

The world teaches us to fight fire with fire. But God teaches us to fight darkness with light. *"Kill them with kindness"* doesn't mean allow yourself to be mistreated. It means to be intentional about loving others—even when they are hurting. Because oftentimes, people hurt us not out of malice, but because they are suffering

THE BATTLE WITHIN THE MIND

emotionally, mentally, or spiritually. Being kind costs nothing. Being hateful can cost everything.

When your thoughts begin to spiral, pause, and ask: *Have I invited God into this thought? Am I feeding my fear or feeding my faith? What would God want me to do with this emotion?* Your mind doesn't have to be a battlefield—it can become a sanctuary. Let God renew your thoughts and restore your peace.

CHAPTER 4:

HEALING THE INNER CHILD AND BREAKING THE CYCLE

> *"He heals the brokenhearted and binds up their wounds." – Psalm 147:3*

I never realized how much our childhood shaped us until I became a mother myself. Like many of us, I once said, "I'll never do this when I have kids," but I found myself doing exactly that. Not because I wanted to—but because I didn't know any other way.

That's when it hit me: I wasn't just parenting my children, I was also parenting my past. We often talk about breaking generational curses, but rarely do we pause to ask:

HEALING THE INNER CHILD AND BREAKING THE CYCLE

What exactly is a generational curse?

To me, it's a pattern—a cycle of pain, dysfunction, silence, or survival—that gets passed down from one generation to the next. These patterns aren't just physical or behavioral; they're deeply emotional and spiritual. Sometimes what we call *"personality"* is protection. And sometimes what we call *"independence"* is unhealed abandonment.

These curses, these cycles, are rooted in our inner child, the little version of us who experienced life before we had the words to process it. When that child doesn't feel loved, safe, seen, or nurtured, they carry that wound into adulthood. And that wound becomes the foundation for how we love, trust, and live.

Your inner child isn't just a cute metaphor, it's the part of you that holds onto your earliest emotional experiences. It's the version of you that still remembers the rejection, the silence, the yelling, or the emotional distance. And while time moves forward, your inner child stays frozen in those moments until you return to bring healing. When we don't address the needs of our inner child, those unmet needs don't just disappear—they evolve.

HEALING THE INNER CHILD AND BREAKING THE CYCLE

They show up as emotional shutdown, fear of abandonment, people-pleasing, difficulty trusting others, and even the inability to ask for help.

My inner child was missing that emotional piece of the puzzle. That missing piece caused me years of pain and suffering. Most of the time, it wasn't anyone else's fault but my own. My wounded inner child had a deep fear of being abandoned, of depending on others, and of being emotionally vulnerable.

Because of that, I struggled to maintain healthy relationships—not because I didn't want them, but because I didn't know how. I couldn't fully show up as a parent for my children—not because I didn't love them, but because I wasn't connected to myself. I didn't realize that part of me—the little girl inside—was still waiting for love, reassurance, and safety. And so, I continued the cycle. Until God interrupted it.

There came a point where I had to stop blaming my parents. I had to stop waiting for apologies and start searching for understanding. I realized my parents weren't just "Mom and Dad"—they were people.

HEALING THE INNER CHILD AND BREAKING THE CYCLE

People with their own traumas, their own unmet needs, and their own inner children that had never been seen either. It doesn't excuse the pain, but it explains the pattern. And in that realization, I found grace. It was then I began to forgive—not just them, but myself. And in that forgiveness, I started to heal. God didn't just want me to survive the past. He wanted me to redeem it. So, I invited Him in. I began nurturing my inner child by affirming what she never heard:

"I am enough." "I am worthy of love." "I am safe to feel." "I don't have to carry this alone."

Healing didn't happen overnight, and even now I still have my moments. But I keep showing up. I keep praying. I keep asking God to hold me while I hold the little girl inside of me.

As parents, we often focus on the basics—food, shelter, and discipline. But sometimes we forget the most crucial part: love. Deep, present, unconditional love. My parents taught me hard work, maturity, manners, and responsibility. For that, I am grateful. But I never learned how to be soft. I didn't understand emotional closeness, or what it meant to truly receive love—not the kind

HEALING THE INNER CHILD AND BREAKING THE CYCLE

that's earned, but the kind that's freely given. And because I didn't see that growing up, I struggled to offer it in my own home. My kids didn't need a perfect mom. They needed a present one. A healed one.

I remember one conversation with my husband that changed everything. He said, *"I don't know how to explain it, but I feel like you sometimes self-sabotage."* At first, it hurt. But then I realized—that was God speaking through him. It was the wake-up call I didn't know I needed. I had been so busy protecting myself from pain that I didn't realize I was also blocking love. That moment became my turning point.

I prayed: *"Create in me a clean heart, O God, and renew a right spirit within me." —Psalm 51:10*

And then I started the work. I began therapy. I started journaling. I started asking God not just to heal me—but to reparent me. To teach me what love looks like through His eyes.

Breaking generational curses aren't about doing better. It's about going deeper. It's about confronting what has been hidden and choosing

HEALING THE INNER CHILD AND BREAKING THE CYCLE

to love the parts of yourself that once felt unlovable. You are not responsible for the pain you inherited, but you are responsible for the healing. Your inner child deserves tenderness. Your future family deserves peace. And your heart deserves the kind of love that only God can give.

So, start where you are. Let God meet you there. And take His hand as you break the cycle—one prayer, one truth, one brave step at a time.

CHAPTER 5:

MAKING PEACE WITH THE PAST

> *"Forget the former things; do not dwell on the past. See, I am doing a new thing!"* – Isaiah 43:18-19

Before my husband, I remember very vividly, crying with my head buried face down in the pillow as I desperately asked God to make the pain stop and to bring me peace. Sleeping next to someone and feeling so unloved, unseen, and unsafe—not because they were bad people, but because I was beginning to transform into someone who no longer fit comfortably in the relationship. It was this moment that I took my transformation with God more seriously, because I knew it was His

MAKING PEACE WITH THE PAST

way of saying, *"Put Me first and I shall show you the way."* And He did just that. He brought me peace, happiness, and hope.

Making peace with the past doesn't mean pretending it didn't happen. It means facing it, feeling it, and forgiving it. It's about learning to look back without staying stuck. Peace is not found in ignoring pain—it's found in surrendering it. Making peace means no longer allowing your past to dictate your present or steal your future.

I used to think peace would come when everyone apologized or made things right. But real peace came when I stopped waiting for closure from people and started seeking clarity through God. I realized peace wasn't something the world could give—it was something only God could restore within me.

We all make mistakes. I've done and said things I regret. Before God transformed my heart, I lived impulsively—forming meaningless connections, making reckless decisions, and seeking validation in all the wrong places. I was attracting emotionally unavailable people because I was emotionally disconnected from myself.

MAKING PEACE WITH THE PAST

I justified the chaos—cutting people off, lashing out, blaming others for my pain. It wasn't until I met someone who mirrored every unhealed part of me that I understood the depth of my brokenness. That relationship became the wake-up call I didn't know I needed. When it ended, I experienced a heartbreak so deep, I knew only God could reach that place and heal it.

That heartbreak wasn't punishment—it was preparation. God used it to pull me closer. He whispered, *"Surrender your heart to Me, and I will show you who you really are."* And He did. I began journaling, reflecting, and praying more deeply than ever before. As painful as it was, I needed to see the role I played in my own suffering. God walked me through a hard truth: I needed to make peace not just with others, but with myself.

I began to forgive myself and the people I had hurt. I reached out to those still in my life, and I released the ones who were no longer meant to be a part of my life. I learned that not all relationships are meant to last forever—some are meant to teach us. And once we learn the lesson, it's okay to move on. I let go of the shame, the guilt, and the people who reminded me of who I used to be.

MAKING PEACE WITH THE PAST

And in letting go, I found my peace. The kind of peace that brings rest, clarity, and joy—not from perfection, but from purpose.

As I healed, God began to surround me with people who reflected the light I was stepping into. I met my husband during this time—a season when I was no longer searching to be saved, but willing to be seen. That's when I learned: what I once thought was love, was survival. What I have now is divine alignment.

When we finally release what we thought we needed, God makes room for what we truly deserve. And sometimes, peace is the gift we receive after choosing obedience.

"Come to Me, all who are weary and burdened, and I will give you rest." – Matthew 11:28

Reflective Question: What part of your past are you still carrying that God is asking you to release?

CHAPTER 6:

OVERCOMING NEGATIVE THOUGHTS THROUGH GOD'S TRUTH

> *"Do not be conformed to this world, but be transformed by the renewing of your mind..."*— Romans 12:2

Let's be honest—negative thoughts don't just appear out of nowhere. They're often rooted in past pain, unhealed trauma, and insecurities we've yet to confront. Sometimes they're triggered by the enemy, who whisper lies meant to distort our identity. And other times, it's just our minds playing tricks on us. Negative thoughts are like weeds—they grow fast if they're left unchecked. But affirmations?

OVERCOMING NEGATIVE THOUGHTS THROUGH GOD'S TRUTH

They're seeds. And with time, intention, and prayer, they bloom into belief. We don't speak affirmations because we feel good—we speak them until we do.

The truth is negative thoughts will always exist. Even when you love God. Even when you've forgiven others. Even when you're doing everything "right." Our bond with God was never meant to protect us from hardship—it was meant to sustain us through it. That bond reminds us that peace isn't found in our minds; it's found in Him.

Have you ever thought, *"I'm not enough"?* Let me remind you: our Savior died on the cross because you were. Despite your flaws. Despite your mistakes. Despite your overthinking. That kind of love should remind you how valuable you truly are.

Negative thoughts left unchecked lead to negative actions. They pull us out of alignment with God's will. They cause us to speak with bitterness, act with anger, or isolate in shame. That's why we must replace every lie with truth. Every doubt with a declaration. Every fear with faith.

OVERCOMING NEGATIVE THOUGHTS THROUGH GOD'S TRUTH

Affirmation: "I have the mind of Christ. I am loved, seen, and chosen."

When we practice thinking positively, our patience expands. Our resilience grows. And suddenly, the things that once disturb our peace no longer hold the same power. That's the beauty of renewing the mind. And yes—it takes work. But it gets easier with practice.

Try this: Every time your thoughts start spiraling, **take a deep breath in** *(smell the birthday cake)* **then exhale slowly** *(blow out the candles)***.**

Then pray: *"Lord, I come to You asking that You replace these negative thoughts with Your truth. Help me to see myself as You do. Help me to believe in Your promises, and not in my fears. I am who You say I am. Not what my insecurities whisper. Not what my mind assumes. I trust You. In Jesus' name, Amen."*

You see, it's okay to pause. It's okay to pray. And it's more than okay to ask for help. God never gets tired of hearing your voice. You're not bothering Him. You're building intimacy with Him.

OVERCOMING NEGATIVE THOUGHTS THROUGH GOD'S TRUTH

Affirmation: "My thoughts are being transformed by God's Word. I release what doesn't serve me."

Often, it's not the situation—it's our interpretation that stirs chaos. How many times have you seen something, assumed, and treated that assumption like it was fact? I've done it more times than I can count. That's why we must lean not on our own understanding but trust in God's.

"Trust in the Lord with all your heart and lean not on your own understanding..." — Proverbs 3:5

The devil is an expert manipulator. He distorts perspectives, fuels overthinking, and builds division in our relationships—especially when we rely more on our emotions than God's truth. To overcome this, we need to stay grounded: journaling, praying, meditating, and surrounding ourselves with light. Sometimes the state of our mind reflects how we're treating our body. When we're unkept—when we stop grooming, eating well, or caring for ourselves, it becomes easier to believe we're not worthy.

**OVERCOMING NEGATIVE THOUGHTS
THROUGH GOD'S TRUTH**

But when we dress up, speak life, and care for ourselves, our spirit rises with our appearance.

Affirmation: "I am worthy. I am whole. I choose peace."

Negative thoughts may come, but they don't have to stay. With God, we can transform our minds—one truth, one breath, one prayer at a time.

CHAPTER 7:

REDEFINING THE SOFT GIRL ERA THROUGH FAITH

> *"Charm is deceptive, and beauty is fleeting; but a woman who fears the Lord is to be praised."*
> *— Proverbs 31:30*

We often use the term *"soft girl era"* without truly defining what it means. On social media, it's glamorized—wrapped in expensive self-care routines, Stanley cups, flawless makeup, and aesthetic content. I used to think that was the standard, too. I believed that to enter my soft girl era, I had to dress in a certain way,

REDEFINING THE SOFT GIRL ERA THROUGH FAITH

buy certain things and look effortlessly polished—because that's what was portrayed. But as I began to walk with God and view life through His eyes, I discovered something deeper: My soft girl era didn't require performance—it required peace.

Through prayer and surrender, I learned that my soft girl era isn't about perfection or performance. It's about living in my truth and becoming my authentic self without fear of judgment. It's about:

- Praying more

- Setting healthy boundaries

- Surrendering the need for constant control

- Allowing myself to be supported by my loved ones and my husband

- Letting God soften the parts of me that the world hardened

"Cast all your anxiety on Him because He cares for you." — 1 Peter 5:7

REDEFINING THE SOFT GIRL ERA THROUGH FAITH

God began to show me that healing wasn't found in isolation. He showed me that independence is different from disconnection—and that I didn't have to carry everything on my own. Society teaches us *to "be your own everything"* or *"do bad all by yourself."* But the truth is: You weren't meant to live guarded, disconnected, or alone.

Before God, I kept people at arm's length. Closeness was weakness. I feared being hurt again, so I never let anyone in. I associated vulnerability with being clingy, desperate, or naïve. But God revealed something to me: Not everyone is here to hurt you.

When we stay guarded too long, we become cold. We start to project the very pain we were trying to protect ourselves from. God, in His love, wants to heal those broken places—not just so we can feel good, but so we can give and receive love fully.

"Above all, love each other deeply, because love covers over a multitude of sins." — 1 Peter 4:8

REDEFINING THE SOFT GIRL ERA THROUGH FAITH

My soft girl era isn't a trend—it's a lifestyle. It's about emotional honesty. It's about surrounding myself with people who uplift, support, and see me. It's about trusting that even if someone lets me down, God never will. Yes, I still get those thoughts: *"What if I get hurt again?" "What if I get let down again?"* But I know this: God has already gone before me. He will protect me. He will remove those who are only meant for a season. And even if something ends, it's not failure—it's a lesson or a blessing. Either way, I still win.

Being guarded is exhausting. It weighs your heart down with fear, suspicion, and anxiety. But putting your faith in God brings peace. He already knows the full story of your life—every chapter, every twist, every ending, and every beginning.

"For I know the plans I have for you," declares the Lord, "plans to prosper you and not to harm you, plans to give you hope and a future." — Jeremiah 29:11

So let people in. Stop bracing yourself for pain that hasn't happened yet. Stop fearing the unknown when you already know the One who holds it all. You don't have to be in control when you're covered by God.

CHAPTER 8:

LOVE, PARTNERSHIP, & FAITH

> *"Love is patient, love is kind. It does not envy, it does not boast, it is not proud."*
> *— 1 Corinthians 13:4*

Lately, I've been doing a lot of soul-searching when it comes to love, especially in my marriage. I used to think love was about the spark, the butterflies, the feel-good moments—but life has taught me that's not the full picture. Real love is something deeper. It is patient, it is kind, and honestly, it's sometimes quiet and still. It doesn't always shout through flowers and grand gestures. Sometimes it whispers through consistency, sacrifice, and grace.

LOVE, PARTNERSHIP, & FAITH

My husband and I entered a season of rediscovery. Having kids changed everything—beautifully, but also drastically. Our roles shifted, time together became limited, and I started to feel disconnected. I questioned everything: *"Do I still love him?" "Are we just coexisting?"* Those questions scared me.

He felt it too. My distance. My silence. And even though he didn't always understand what I was going through, he stayed patient. He kept trying. He kept loving me through it. While I was emotionally withdrawing, he was still praying over us. That hit me deeply. That's when I started to pray even harder. I surrendered control to God and asked for clarity.

With time came clarity, and with clarity came understanding. It wasn't that I didn't love him. It was that my inner child—the part of me that feared abandonment and rejection—had taken over. I went into fight-or-flight mode without realizing it. I unconsciously built walls and emotionally isolated myself as a defense mechanism. That's when God reminded me: love isn't just a feeling; it's a daily choice.

"Above all, love each other deeply, because love covers over a multitude of sins." — *1 Peter 4:8*

LOVE, PARTNERSHIP, & FAITH

My husband and I came from different backgrounds. He shows love through his presence and providing. I need words, affection, and reassurance. We were both loving—just not in each other's language. That's why it's so important to have conversations about love languages and expectations. The enemy often uses miscommunication to create distance, but God brings clarity when we invite Him in.

Love is kind, patient, and safe. It isn't just butterflies and chemistry. Chemistry fades. But real, authentic love—the kind God desires for us—endures. It may get lost in life's chaos, but it always finds its way back when God is at the center. Love is unconditional and never transactional. You shouldn't have to give something to receive love or offer love just to get something in return. That's conditional love, and it isn't of God.

We all need healing in some way or form. And you don't really know where healing is needed until you're triggered. That's why relationships aren't meant to be perfect. They're meant to stretch us, sharpen us, and help us grow.

"Two are better than one... If either of them falls down, one can help the other up." Ecclesiastes 4:9-10

LOVE, PARTNERSHIP, & FAITH

They say the right person will change you. But really, the right person will reveal the parts of you that need changing. And that's when you choose: to either work through those wounds or let them destroy what's good. Many relationships fall apart because it's easier to walk away than it is to work through discomfort. But when God is the center, you learn that discomfort is not always danger—it can be the beginning of transformation.

Love is choosing your partner every day—even on the days they can't give you 100%. It's standing beside them through their battles, supporting them as they navigate their own wounds. It's choosing grace over criticism, understanding over assumption.

We all lacked something in childhood that affects us today. That's why marriage vows include "for better or worse." There will always be something that triggers us. And that's where partnership, patience, and grace come into play. You learn to show up for each other, not just in celebration but also in struggle.

"Let all that you do be done in love." — 1 Corinthians 16:14

LOVE, PARTNERSHIP, & FAITH

Being with my husband has taught me that true love requires seeing someone fully—even their flaws—and still choosing to stay. It's not always sunshine and rainbows. When love is based on what a person does for you or how they make you feel, it will disappear when the conditions change. That isn't love. That's lust. And lust is not from God.

Love means letting down your walls. Love means compromise. Love means sacrifice. But most importantly, love means God is in the middle. I've come to realize that the key to a healthy marriage is a strong relationship with God. He restores what is broken. He strengthens our faith. He heals our hearts and gives us hope. God helped me and my husband to see that we were stuck in the roommate phase and the love was absent—but it wasn't gone. It was buried under exhaustion, stress, and unmet needs. With

God's help, we're digging it back up. And we're rebuilding, not from the surface, but from the soul.

If you're in that place right now, I want to tell you: love doesn't die easily. It may go quiet, but when you water it with intention, prayer, and God's grace, it blooms

CHAPTER 9:

PARENTING FROM A HEALED PLACE

> *"Start children off on the way they should go, and even when they are old they will not turn from it." — Proverbs 22:6*

Parenting is one of the most sacred callings—and one of the most revealing. The moment we choose to bring life into this world, we assume the responsibility of nurturing, guiding, and shaping another human being. But what if we're still learning how to nurture and guide ourselves? What if we're still healing? We've all heard the saying, *"Our kids didn't ask to be here."* That truth comes with weight. Being a parent isn't about putting food on the table or keeping clothes on their backs.

PARENTING FROM A HEALED PLACE

It's about showing love, being patient, offering emotional safety, and being present. Those things aren't automatic. They're learned—and often learned the hard way. Especially if you weren't raised in a home or environment where emotional connection or healthy communication was modeled. That's where healing begins. Our healing becomes their foundation.

Before I became a mother, I was emotionally grounded and rarely anxious. But pregnancy changed that. My hormones triggered emotional imbalance. I cried more. I worried more. I felt more. And after giving birth, those feelings intensified. I was overwhelmed, easily triggered, and emotionally withdrawn—and I didn't know why. It wasn't until I started drafting this book that.

I realized: motherhood doesn't just bring life into the world—it resurrects your past. It pulls forward buried pain, forcing you to confront wounds you didn't know were still open. Our hormones don't create new wounds; awaken the ones we've buried. My wounded inner child had never fully healed, and motherhood magnified that truth.

PARENTING FROM A HEALED PLACE

Signs that your inner child may still be wounded include:

- Overreacting emotionally to small situations

- Struggling with rejection or abandonment

- Hypervigilance and chronic anxiety

- Difficulty forming close emotional bonds

- Inability to express or receive love without discomfort

- Emotional withdrawal during stress

    I started noticing these signs in myself—especially after having children. I found myself wondering why my kids clung to their dad more than me. It hurt. I began to feel like I had failed as a mother. But through prayer, reflection, and honest conversations with God, I realized something powerful: my husband and I were raised differently. He was given emotional space as a child—to express, to feel, to be heard. I wasn't. Naturally, our children gravitated toward the parent who offered the emotional environment they instinctively craved. Not because I didn't love them, but because

PARENTING FROM A HEALED PLACE

I didn't heal enough to love them in the way they needed. That realization didn't destroy me—it liberated me. I stopped seeing myself as a failure and started seeing myself as a work in progress. I began to pray more, reflect deeper, and take intentional steps toward emotional healing.

It is important to establish a strong relationship with God. Without God, I wouldn't have had the clarity to understand what was happening within me. I would have continued the generational curse and allowed trauma to seep into my relationship with my kids. Then my children would have grown up with wounds of their own. The change starts with you. Don't let old phrases like *"you gone spoil that baby"* stop you from loving on your kids. Children aren't spoiled by love. They're spoiled by a lack of boundaries and consistency—not by affection or emotional responsiveness.

Have you ever heard of Erikson's stages of psychosocial development? His theory outlines crucial stages of emotional growth. During infancy, the stage is "Trust vs. Mistrust. "If a child learns their caregivers are dependable and nurturing, they develop emotional security. If not, mistrust and insecurity take root.

PARENTING FROM A HEALED PLACE

This is often where the wounded inner child begins. For toddlers and adolescents, Erikson identifies "Autonomy vs. Shame and Doubt" and "Identity vs. Confusion." These stages help shape independence, confidence, and identity. If children are emotionally neglected or overly criticized, they carry shame and confusion into adulthood, something I experienced firsthand. Understanding Erikson's theory gave me language for what I was feeling and clarity on how to better show up for my children. Our responses shape their worldview. Our healing helps them build healthy emotional foundations.

I come from a family that rarely gathered unless tragedy brought us together. Holidays weren't filled with joy and laughter. I didn't realize how much that affected me until I had children. Now, I long to create a kind of home where holidays are joyful, family time is sacred, and love is always present. I want my kids to experience the warmth and security I once missed.

Parenting from a healed place doesn't mean you won't make mistakes—it means you're willing to grow through them. You pause before you react. You apologize when you mess up. You teach through grace and humility.

PARENTING FROM A HEALED PLACE

You intentionally show up. I remember when I started to wake up at 4:30 a.m. to cook dinner and clean the house. Instead of doing these things after work and school, I shifted my routine to be more present with my kids. Whether we were building blocks or sitting on the floor sharing snacks, being a part of their world mattered. That simple, intentional act made a difference, and I could see it in their smiles and eyes.

Kids don't need perfection. They need presence. They need safe arms, listening ears, and consistent love. They need to see what healing looks like, so they don't have to start from scratch. So, we break the cycle—not just for us, but for them.

Isaiah 66:13 says, "As a mother comforts her child, so will I comfort you."

That's the kind of mother I want to be—the kind that brings comfort, connection, and healing through God's grace.

Reflective Question: What unhealed parts of yourself are surfacing through your parenting, and how can you begin to nurture your inner child so you can better nurture your own?

CHAPTER 10:

WHEN GOD HOLDS UP THE MIRROR

> *"There is a time for everything, and a season for every activity under the heavens."* Ecclesiastes 3:1

One thing I've learned on this journey is that God doesn't whisper when He's trying to shift you—He speaks through patterns, people, and even pain. When it's time to change, He'll let you know. And if you don't listen the first time, the lesson will get louder until it grabs your attention.

We pray for growth, healing, and transformation, but we don't always realize what we're asking for. Growth requires discomfort.

WHEN GOD HOLDS UP THE MIRROR

Healing takes confrontation. Transformation demands action. God won't just hand us what we're praying for—He'll equip us to receive it and test us to see if we're truly ready. Step one is acknowledging our flaws, insecurities, and patterns. Step two is praying for the strength, clarity, and wisdom to change. But step three—the one we skip the most—is putting in the work. You can't ask for peace and keep running toward chaos. You can't ask for change and keep living in the same cycle. When you ask God for patience, don't be surprised if He places you in situations that test your patience. If you ask for financial discipline, He'll give you moments where you'll have to say no to your wants to honor your needs. It's not punishment—it's preparation.

Have you ever noticed how the same thing keeps happening over and over? Ever found yourself thinking, "Why is this happening again?"

That's because God will give you the same lesson until you learn what He's trying to teach you. He continuously mirrors our flaws through people and situations. I used to think I was the perfect girlfriend—that any man would be lucky to have me. I'm smart, beautiful, ambitious, God-

WHEN GOD HOLDS UP THE MIRROR

fearing, and goal driven. I have a career, I'm financially responsible, and I can cook and clean.

So, in my mind, I was "wifey material. "But God humbled me. He showed me that I was also selfish, condescending, emotionally unavailable, dismissive, and overly independent. Those are not the qualities of a wife or a true partner. That realization was a hard pill to swallow.

When you're faced with the truth, your ego takes a hit. At first, I believed I didn't deserve love or good things. I thought I was a bad person. But God reminded me: I am not a bad person. I am a good person with unhealthy habits. And habits can be changed.

God also uses people as mirrors. You'll start noticing yourself in others—the good, the bad, and the unhealed. He's not being cruel. He's being intentional. He wants you to recognize the parts of yourself that need to be surrendered. Until you break the pattern, the pattern will repeat.

Through prayer and surrender, I began to give myself grace. I accepted my flaws, not to hide them—but to correct them. I leaned on God

WHEN GOD HOLDS UP THE MIRROR

to hold me up as I confronted and fought the spiritual forces that had shaped my mindset and behaviors.

We often blame others or circumstances for our pain, but sometimes we are the ones holding ourselves back. Not because we're bad people, but because we're trying to live life on our own terms instead of God's plan. And anytime we step outside of God's will, confusion and chaos follow. But the beauty in God's timing is that it's never too late. Even when we delay. Even when we detour. When God says it's time—He'll open the door, but it's up to us to walk through it. Obedience is how we show we're ready.

If you are in a season where everything feels uncertain, ask yourself: Is this a shift God is calling me to make? And if so, am I resisting the change or preparing for it?

Trust that if God is calling you to grow, He's already given you everything you need to get there. It's your move now.

CHAPTER 11:

LIFE AFTER CHRIST

> *"And we know that in all things God works for the good of those who love him, who have been called according to his purpose." — Romans 8:28*

When people say, "It gets better with time," they often forget the most important part—it only truly gets better when you're walking with Christ. Time alone doesn't heal wounds; it's God who brings restoration. Life after Christ doesn't mean your struggles stop, but it means your perspective changes. You begin to see challenges not as punishments but as preparation.

LIFE AFTER CHRIST

Living a life in Christ means walking with resilience, discipline, intention, and awareness. It means being rooted in something stronger than yourself—leaning on God's strength when yours runs out. When I accepted Christ as the center of my life, everything shifted. I began to navigate hardships with a new mindset. I stopped asking 'why me?' and started asking 'what is God trying to show me?'

Life doesn't pause for our pain. There is no stop button when the world feels heavy. But God teaches us how to take things one day at a time. When I was in nursing school, life didn't stop for me. I became pregnant—twice—during my program. I had to sit out a semester to give birth, and just two weeks before another term ended, I gave birth again. Two days later, I was back in class taking an exam.

Do you know how hard it is to focus after pushing out a 7-pound baby, running on no sleep, nursing a newborn, and caring for a toddler? I had to pray just to make it through. The night before the test, I prayed for clarity. On the morning of the exam, I prayed again. I asked God to sharpen my mind—and He did. By His grace, I passed that exam and moved on to the next course.

LIFE AFTER CHRIST

God has always provided what I needed, even when I had nothing. There were days when I had overdrafts in my bank account and no idea how I would make ends meet. Instead of focusing on the lack, I focused on the blessings I did have healthy children, food on our table, a supportive partner and family. I trusted God to fill in the gaps—and He did. He blessed me with school scholarships that covered my tuition and gave me enough extra to pay my bills. He provided an internship job that allowed me to make my own schedule. Every time I thought I was at my breaking point; God gave me strength to keep going. That is what life after Christ looks like—leaning into God even when life leans hard on you.

"The Lord is my strength and my shield; my heart trusts in him, and he helps me." — Psalm 28:7

Now, I'm walking proof of God's faithfulness. I finished nursing school. I published my first healing journal. I wrote my first book. And most importantly, I found my purpose. I'm no longer afraid of failure or bound by the opinions of others. I take risks, trust the process, and I know who holds my future.

LIFE AFTER CHRIST

So, what does it really mean to live life after Christ?

It means you walk with vision and not just sight. You move with purpose and not just emotion. You make decisions rooted in prayer and not fear. It's not that the storms stop—it's that you're anchored through them.

> *"Therefore, if anyone is in Christ, the new creation has come: The old has gone, the new is here!" — 2 Corinthians 5:17*

Living life after Christ is a daily decision to choose faith over fear. It's the understanding that everything you face is working together for your good. It's knowing that setbacks are setups, and that nothing is wasted in God's hands.

If you're wondering how to begin living life in Christ, start by inviting Him into your everyday moments. Talk to Him in prayer. Read His Word. Let His voice be the loudest one in your life. Surround yourself with people who push you closer to God. Take intentional steps daily, even if they're small. The transformation doesn't happen overnight, but each step brings you closer to peace, purpose, and fulfillment.

LIFE AFTER CHRIST

Friend, I don't know what your storm looks like. But I do know this—God is not done with you. He has plans for you, purposes for you, and healing waiting for you. Keep your eyes on Him and let Him lead you into your next chapter. Life after Christ isn't easier—but it's richer, deeper, and more meaningful.

CHAPTER 12

SPEAK LIFE: THE POWER OF OUR WORDS

"Say only what you mean. Speak truth with love." — Don Miguel Ruiz, The Four Agreements

> *"Do not let any unwholesome talk come out of your mouths, but only what is helpful for building others up according to their needs, that it may benefit those who listen." — Ephesians 4:29*

There was a time in my life when I spoke from pain instead of peace. I didn't always recognize it, but my words were often sharp, guarded, or full of doubt.

SPEAK LIFE: THE POWER OF OUR WORDS

I had learned to speak from defense—because for so long, I had been on the receiving end of harmful words.

Growing up, I was often criticized for my appearance. Whether it came from family, people who I thought were my friends, or from my high school boyfriend, those remarks didn't just sting—they stuck.

Over time, I unknowingly internalized those words and started speaking them over myself. Even in the mirror, I'd criticize what I saw. I didn't need anyone else to tear me down—I had taken over the job. I doubted compliments, rejected encouragement, and dismissed anything kind as a lie. I had learned to speak death over myself, not life. But when I gave my heart to Christ, everything began to shift. God began working on the words I used—not just toward others, but especially toward myself.

"The tongue has the power of life and death, and those who love it will eat its fruit." — Proverbs 18:21 (NIV)

I realized how powerful words are. They can build bridges or burn them. They can heal or

SPEAK LIFE: THE POWER OF OUR WORDS

destroy. And we don't just hurt others with our words—we also hurt ourselves when we gossip, criticize, or speak in dishonesty. Being impeccable with your word means speaking from a place of wholeness and honesty. It means refusing to speak out of bitterness, even when you're justified in your pain. It means not using your voice as a weapon but as a tool for peace.

As a mother, I'm now even more intentional with my words. I know my children are listening, and not just to what I say to them—but also what I say about myself. If they hear me speaking life, speaking the truth, and speaking kindly about others, they'll grow up knowing the standard. But if they hear me tearing myself or others down, they'll think that's normal. I want to model words that build, not break.

Being impeccable with your word also means saying what you mean but doing so in love. There were times when I avoided honesty because I didn't want to hurt feelings—but that wasn't integrity. And there were times when I told the truth with no grace, which is just as harmful. Through God, I've learned the balance: speak truth but wrap it in love.

SPEAK LIFE: THE POWER OF OUR WORDS

"Instead, speaking the truth in love, we will grow to become in every respect the mature body of him who is the head, that is, Christ." — *Ephesians 4:15 (NIV)*

Now, I try to pause before I speak. I ask: *Is it true? Is it kind? Is it necessary?* If not, I stay silent. Because silence can be more healing than reckless speech. And sometimes, the most powerful thing you can do is speak a word of encouragement—to yourself or to someone else—right in the middle of chaos.

So many of us are still carrying words spoken over us years ago. The good ones gave us wings. The bad ones left bruises. Let this be your reminder: your words matter. Speak carefully. Speak prayerfully. Speak with grace. Because when you choose to be impeccable with your word, you reflect the heart of God. And that kind of speech? That's power, healing, and freedom all wrapped in one.

CHAPTER 13:

WHEN THEIR WORDS DON'T DEFINE YOU

"Nothing others do is because of you."
– Don Miguel Ruiz, The Four Agreements

> *"Am I now trying to win the approval of human beings, or of God? Or am I trying to please people? If I were still trying to please people, I would not be a servant of Christ." — Galatians 1:10*

There was a time in my life when the opinions of others felt like a final verdict on who I was. A rude comment could send me into a spiral. Rejection—whether subtle or loud—made me question my worth. Praise validated me, but the absence of it left me feeling unseen and uncertain.

WHEN THEIR WORDS DON'T DEFINE YOU

I lived constantly on edge, tying my identity to the words and reactions of other people.

As I grew up, that emotional dependence deepened. My family's comments about my appearance and weight, even if disguised as jokes, left wounds that lingered. But the most damaging experience came in high school—when my boyfriend at the time made a habit of tormenting me about my looks. He'd pick apart everything from my face to my figure, comparing me to others in a way that made me feel small and inadequate. I stayed quiet, hoping that if I looked better, acted better, or just stayed loyal, he'd change.

But instead, I changed—and not in a good way. I stopped believing compliments, even when they were genuine. I doubted my beauty, my value, and whether anyone could truly love me without criticism attached. His words echoed louder than the truth, and I carried that insecurity into adulthood. But God doesn't want us to live chained to someone else's brokenness.

"Fear of man will prove to be a snare, but whoever trusts in the Lord is kept safe." — Proverbs 29:25 (NIV)

WHEN THEIR WORDS DON'T DEFINE YOU

Through my walk with Christ, I learned one of the most freeing lessons: what others say or do is not a reflection of me—it's a reflection of them. Their insults, silence, or even praise come from their own lens, shaped by pain, fear, and life experience.

It's not personal—it's projection. This truth didn't come easily. We all want to be seen, loved, and valued. So, when people criticize us or treat us unfairly, it stings. But healing began when I stopped assigning my identity to their behavior. I stopped letting wounded people define a whole and chosen woman. I began anchoring my worth in the Word, not the world. I started to unlearn lies and speak truth over myself daily.

"For we are God's masterpiece. He has created us anew in Christ Jesus, so we can do the good things he planned for us long ago." — Ephesians 2:10 (NLT)

Now, when someone projects their insecurities onto me, I pause, pray, and release. I remind myself: "This isn't about me." I no longer take rudeness personally. I no longer internalize silence as rejection. And while compliments are appreciated, I no longer depend on them to feel seen.

WHEN THEIR WORDS DON'T DEFINE YOU

That doesn't mean I accept mistreatment or ignore red flags. It means I don't allow those experiences to poison my self-worth.

I've learned to guard my heart, not harden it.

> *"Above all else, guard your heart, for everything you do flows from it." — Proverbs 4:23 (NIV)*

I've also learned to hold praise and criticism with the same steady hand. My identity isn't built on applause—it's rooted in God's truth. When you live from a place of identity instead of insecurity, you don't need others to validate what God already confirmed.

I remember sitting in my car, parked in the quiet flipping through the pages of my proof copy—this very book you're holding now. What I expected to be the final round of proofreading turned into something deeper. A divine interruption

As I reviewed the words, still uncertain if they were "good enough" I heard a voice in the background—not audibly, but through my phone. Pastor Mike McClure Jr. was preaching live. I had heard this message before, but on this day, it hit me differently. It hit me hard.

WHEN THEIR WORDS DON'T DEFINE YOU

Why? Because I realized I had been quietly disappointed.

I hadn't received the energy, support, or praised I hoped for when I first shared the vision of this book.. or when I announced it was finally published. I was expecting celebration. Validation But instead, I was met with silence, hesitation, or half-hearted congratulations.

And that's when Pastor Mike said something that shook me: We have to grow up and get out of our feelings when we don't get the praise, support, or applause from people who were never assigned to validate what God gave us.

That word spoke directly to my heart. I needed that reminder. Because the truth is—only I know what I've survived

Only I know what God whispered to me.

Only I know the assignment that was placed on my life.

And that's enough.

See, when God gives you a calling,

WHEN THEIR WORDS DON'T DEFINE YOU

He also gives you strength to walk it out—even if no one claps for you. That calling will require your obedience, not their approval. It will require faith, discipline, sacrifice, and solitude.

There will be people—even well-meaning ones—who try to protect you, discourage you, or redirect you... not out of hate, but out of misunderstanding. They can't see what you see. They don't hear what God whispered to you. And that's okay. Don't let their doubt become your delay. Don't let their silence become your surrender.

Like pastor Mike said, you don't need protection when you have Christ and mercy.

That word gave me the push I needed to keep going, And that's why I added this passage here—in real time—hoping it meets the person who needed to hear it too.

Don't give up.

Don't fold because of lack of applause.

Don't let your feelings drown out your faith.

WHEN THEIR WORDS DON'T DEFINE YOU

"So we fix our eyes not on what is seen, but on what is unseen..." — 2 Corinthians 4:18 (NIV)

If you've been shrinking yourself under the weight of others' words, it's time to release it. You are not what they said. You are not what they didn't say. You are who God says you are.

You are enough.
You are chosen.
You are seen.
You are loved.
And no one's opinion can take that away.

Taking your power back begins with one choice: stop taking it personally.
Let their actions reflect where they are—not where you're going.

CHAPTER 14:

ASK, DON'T ASSUME: HEALING THROUGH HONEST COMMUNICATION

"Find the courage to ask questions and express what you really want." — Don Miguel Ruiz, The Four Agreements

> *"Let your conversation be always full of grace, seasoned with salt, so that you may know how to answer everyone." — Colossians 4:6*

One of the greatest sources of unnecessary suffering in my life came from the stories I made up in my head. I would fill in gaps with assumptions, convince myself of things that hadn't been said, and carry silent offenses based on misunderstandings. I thought I was protecting

ASK, DON'T ASSUME: HEALING
THROUGH HONEST COMMUNICATION

myself, but really, I was just isolating my heart. I used to assume someone was mad at me because they didn't respond right away. Or I'd think someone's silence meant they didn't like me. In relationships, I often expected people to know what I needed without me ever expressing it. I assumed love looked a certain way, and if someone didn't show it how I envisioned, I told myself they didn't care.

But the truth is—assumptions are emotional shortcuts that lead us straight into confusion and pain.

Growing up, I learned early on to keep quiet about my needs. Whether it was in family settings, friendships, or dating relationships, I became used to swallowing my feelings. It felt safer to guess than to ask, to hope than to speak. But that silence was costly. It left me feeling unseen and unmet—yet I hadn't given others the chance to understand me in the first place.

Even in my marriage and motherhood journey, I've had to unlearn this habit. I had to become bold enough to say what I need, and graceful enough to listen when others did the

**ASK, DON'T ASSUME: HEALING THROUGH
HONEST COMMUNICATION**

same. I had to trade assumptions for clarity, and fear for communication.

"The purposes of a person's heart are deep waters, but one who has insight draws them out."
— Proverbs 20:5 (NIV)

One of the biggest turning points came when I realized that most of my frustration wasn't caused by what happened—it was caused by what I thought happened. Assumptions had become a way to control situations that made me feel insecure. But in doing so, I robbed myself of connection and peace. God calls us to truth, not to guesswork. He invites us to live openly, honestly, and with intention.

Learning not to make assumptions means asking questions even when it feels awkward. It means pausing to get clarity instead of reacting out of emotion. It means learning to say, *"Hey when you said this, this is what I heard. Is that what you meant?"* or *"I'm feeling a little unsure—can we talk about it?"*

ASK, DON'T ASSUME: HEALING THROUGH HONEST COMMUNICATION

It also means being brave enough to speak your needs—without guilt. That's something I'm still practicing. But every time I say what I truly want, every time I ask instead of assuming, I feel more seen and connected—not just to others, but to myself.

"Therefore each of you must put off falsehood and speak truthfully to your neighbor, for we are all members of one body." — Ephesians 4:25 (NIV)

You don't have to read minds, and you're not responsible for making sure others read yours.

You deserve relationships built on clarity, not confusion. And the only way to get there is through communication rooted in grace.

So, if something feels off, ask.
If you need something, say it.
If you're unsure, seek clarity.

Assumptions create distance. But courage closes the gap.

CHAPTER 15:

DOING YOUR BEST WITH WHAT YOU HAVE

"Just do your best, and you will avoid self-judgment and regret." — Don Miguel Ruiz, The Four Agreements

> *"Whatever you do, work at it with all your heart, as working for the Lord, not for human masters." — Colossians 3:23*

For most of my life, I thought "doing your best" meant doing it all—perfectly, constantly, and without pause. I thought being strong meant showing no weakness, and that giving 100% had to look the same every single day. But life has taught me something softer, something deeper: your best isn't about perfection—it's about presence.

DOING YOUR BEST WITH WHAT YOU HAVE

I've lived through seasons when "my best" looked like getting everything on my to-do list checked off, smiling through exhaustion, being everything to everyone, and still finding time to pray. But there have also been days when my best was just getting out of bed, brushing my hair, and whispering a prayer for strength. And both were valid.

Motherhood taught me that my capacity changes. Nursing school taught me that I can't pour from an empty cup. And my walk with Christ taught me that He doesn't expect perfection—He just asks for obedience and effort.

There were times when I felt guilty for not doing more. Times I cried because I didn't show up the way I wanted to—whether for my kids, my classes, or even myself. But when I look back, I realize I gave what I had in that moment. I did my best with what I had. And that has to be enough.

"My grace is sufficient for you, for my power is made perfect in weakness." — 2 Corinthians 12:9 (NIV)

Doing your best doesn't mean ignoring your limits—it means honoring them. It means waking

DOING YOUR BEST WITH WHAT YOU HAVE

up each day and asking, "What do I have to give today?" and then giving it with love and intention. It means letting go of guilt for what didn't get done and choosing to rest in grace instead. I've learned that regret usually shows up when I pretend, hide, or delay. But when I show up and do my best—honestly, fully, even imperfectly—I can lay my head down in peace, knowing I gave what I could.

Some days, your best will be bold and loud. Other days, it will be quiet and slow. Some days, you'll conquer every task. Others, you'll just keep going. And both versions of you are doing something holy.

"Let us not become weary in doing good, for at the proper time we will reap a harvest if we do not give up." — Galatians 6:9 (NIV)

Don't let comparison steal your joy. Don't let perfectionism rob your peace. And don't measure yourself by what others are doing. You're on your own path. You've fought battles no one saw. You've overcome storms others couldn't survive. Your best is enough. You are enough.

So, show up. Be present. Give what you can. And let grace carry the rest.

FINAL THOUGHTS- A SACRED SURRENDER

> *"Draw near to God and He will draw near to you." — James 4:8*

If you've made it this far in my book, thank you. Truly. Thank you for journeying through some of the most intimate pieces of my life. Thank you for sitting with my truth, for reflecting on your own, and for being open to the possibility that healing and transformation are possible through God.

My deepest prayer is that these pages remind you that it's never too late to start again. It's never too late to surrender. You don't have to be perfect. You don't have to attend church every Sunday or memorize the Bible from front to back. God is not looking for performance—He's

Final Thoughts — A Sacred Surrender

looking for your heart. Truthfully, some of the most spiritually disconnected people sit in pews every week. God doesn't require polished prayers or rehearsed rituals. He desires honesty. He honors authenticity. And He celebrates when we come to Him just as we are—broken, unsure, hopeful, healing.

Every day I continue to grow in my walk with God. I'm still uncovering pieces of my purpose. I still fall short. I still mess up. But through it all, God loves me. His grace doesn't expire. His mercy doesn't run dry.

If nothing else, let my life be proof that God is real. That He heals. That He restores. I'm not perfect, but I am chosen. I am redeemed. And I am committed to watering my relationship with God the same way I water my healing.

You are worthy of that same love. That same relationship. That same peace. Don't let your past talk you out of your future.

Don't let fear keep you from freedom. If you've been waiting for a sign, this is it: God wants your heart, not your perfection.

Final Thoughts — A Sacred Surrender

I pray you continue to show up for yourself, just as you are. And I pray you invite God into that process. Because with Him, there's nothing you can't overcome.

Until next time—take care of your heart, protect your peace, and never stop healing. You are becoming whole.

Helpful Resources

Below are resources that have supported me in my healing journey. I pray these tools bring you comfort, strength, and clarity as you continue your own path toward wholeness and faith.

Faith & Spiritual Growth

• YouVersion Bible App – Free Bible app with devotionals and prayer plans.

• The Bible Recap Podcast – Helps you read and understand scripture daily.

• She Reads Truth – Faith-based studies and community for women.

Mental & Emotional Wellness

• BetterHelp – Online therapy platform with licensed professionals.

• Faithful Counseling – Christian counseling and therapy support.

• Calm App – Guided meditations, breathing exercises, and sleep stories.

Support Hotlines

• National Mental Health Hotline (US): 866-903-3787

• Postpartum Support International: 1-800-944-4773

• National Domestic Violence Hotline: 1-800-799-7233

Self-Help & Reflection Tools

• FAITH JOURNALING: A Reflective Journal for Healing, Growth, & Spiritual Renewal – Companion Journal by Tyeisha Kones. — Amazon.com

• The Four Agreements by Don Miguel Ruiz – A powerful book on personal freedom and inner peace.

Motivational Media

• Steve Harvey Podcast – 'You Have to Get a Little Dirt on You' (https://youtu.be/0DBmDKqAzYQ?si=e56faT-dSCaOp1nh)

• Pastor Mike McClure Jr.—Trust God
https://youtube.com/shorts/0t93Hxe8liY?si=s4MCIgGIZSX89hYR

About the Author

Tyeisha Kones is a nurse, wife, mother of two, and a woman of faith who has walked through pain and come out stronger, wiser, and closer to God. Her personal journey through emotional wounds, motherhood, marriage, and healing inspired her to write this self-help book as a testimony and tool for others.

Tyeisha is passionate about breaking generational cycles, nurturing the inner child, and empowering others to seek faith-led transformation. Her writing speaks from the heart—vulnerable, honest, and deeply rooted in her lived experiences. Through her books and journals, she aims to provide a safe space for healing, growth, and self-reflection, especially for women who have been silenced by life's battles but are ready to rediscover their voice.

Acknowledgements

First, I thank God—the Author of my story and the Voice behind every faithful whisper that carried me through. Without Him, this book would not exist. His grace, patience, and love have been my anchor in every storm and my strength in every breakthrough.

To **my husband, Jerry**, thank you for being my covering. Your quiet strength, your unwavering belief in me, and your love—even in my most fragile moments—kept me grounded. Thank you for choosing me daily.

To **my beautiful children**, you are my light and motivation. Every page of this book was written with you in mind. I pray you always grow up knowing the power of healing, the safety of faith, and the beauty of becoming whole.

To **my family and friends** who saw me, believed in me, and prayed for me—thank you. Your words of encouragement and support gave me courage when I felt overwhelmed.

To **Pastor Mike McClure Jr.** thank you for being a bold voice of truth, faith, and fire. Your words have met me in moments of doubt and silence, giving me the courage to keep moving in purpose even when applause was absent.

The sermon that reminded me I don't need protection when I have Christ and mercy became a divine confirmation that helped push this book into the world. Thank you for walking in your assignment—it made it easier for me to walk in mine

To **every woman** who picks up this book—thank you for trusting me with your heart. I pray these pages remind you that you are not alone, that healing is holy, and that God is always near.

Lastly, to the version of me who didn't give up—thank you for holding on, for listening to God, and for writing even when it hurt.

With love and gratitude,

Tyeisha Kones